-British WARSHIPS
Since 1945

by Mike Critchley

(Part 2)

£1.80

By Vice-Admiral Sir John Roxburgh,
KCB, CBE, DXO, DSC*
Flag Officer Sea Training — 1967-1969
Flag Officer Plymouth — 1969
Flag Officer Submarines — 1969-1972

THE SUBMARINE SERVICE
SINCE 1945

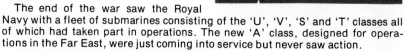

This book covers submarines, depot ships and repair ships since 1945, concluding with the Porpoise class of conventional submarine. The vital break through of nuclear power — which has so transformed the submarine from a vessel of relative immobility to the capital ship of to-day — is dealt with elsewhere.

The end of the war saw the Royal Navy with a fleet of submarines consisting of the 'U', 'V', 'S' and 'T' classes all of which had taken part in operations. The new 'A' class, designed for operations in the Far East, were just coming into service but never saw action.

All these submarines were technically similar to those of the inter-war years in propulsion and armament. German wartime developments of the snorkel and the high capacity long endurance Type XXI battery drive U-boats were yet to be developed in our fleet. The main armament was the Mk 8 torpedo and submarines mounted either the 3" or 4" gun. Action Information equipment was still comparatively primitive, relying mainly on the skill of the Commanding Officer using the periscope, aided by the "Fruit Machine" calculator and with some basic information provided by the sonar operator (or asidic operator as he was then known). The advantages provided by the advent of radar had yet to be felt to any degree.

Immediate post-war developements saw the fitting of the snorkel (or snort as we know it), and centemetric radar. These were followed by the 'T' Conversion submarine, whereby certain of the 'T' class were cut in half, lengthened, streamlined with the gun removed and fitted with enhanced battery power to given them similar performance to the German Type XXI. Anti-submarine warfare, which became the primary role for our submarines, highlighted the requirement for ultra quiet underwater performance and thus for good underwater streamlining. This, in 1955, saw the removal of the gun from the 'A' class and the streamlining of their bridge and superstructure. Sonar developments to match this role continued in both the active and passive mode and advances in the Action Information Organisation also took place with improved calculators to assist the Commanding Officer.

The ultimate fulfilment of our post-war conventional submarine designs took shape in the 8 Porpoise class submarines — followed by their 13 improved sisters of the Oberon class — which joined the fleet between 1958 and 1964. These submarines were arguably the quietest and most advanced conventional submarines of their day in the world. They also formed the basis of the Australian and Canadian submarine forces.

Development of the German 'Walther' design High Test Peroxide power unit also took place in the 1950's with the building of two experimental submarines, Explorer and Excalibur. These possessed greatly enhanced underwater performance in speed and endurance over conventional battery powered submarines. However the advent of nuclear power overtook developments in the HTP field which were therefore abandoned.

Submarine depot ships afloat at the end of the war consisted of the modern ship Adamant together with the sister ships Forth and Maidstone. The fleet repair ship Tyne (sister ship to the Adamant) was also in service and was later

2

to become a submarine depot ship. The converted Canadian Pacific passenger liners Montclare and Wolf augmented submarine depot ship strength during the war and in the early days of peace. Other ships which performed a repair ship and submarine depot ship role were the converted Cunard liner Ausonia based in Malta, and the converted landing ship (tank) Narvik at Londonderry and later in Malta.

Submarine Squadrons (or Flotillas as they were then called) in the United Kingdom were based on depot ships at Rothesay in the Clyde and at Portland, and ashore at Fort Blockhouse, Gosport. Abroad we had submarines in Malta (later to be based on a depot ship there) and with a depot ship in Hong Kong; this squadron later transferring to Sydney, Australia where in time the Australian submarine arm was formed and our own forces withdrew. Submarines were also based at Halifax, Nova Scotia to assist with the anti-submarine training of the Canadian Navy and in the development of the Canadian submarine service. During 'confrontation' with Indonesia we had submarines operating from the Naval Base at Singapore. These overseas submarine squadrons were in general married accompanied appointments and were highly popular postings, giving personnel the opportunity to see the world in company with their wives and families — alas no longer the case.

As time passed and our overseas commitments were relinquished the submarine service concentrated on the home based. The Rothesay squadron moved with it's depot ship to Faslane, and Faslane and Gosport became our main operational and training bases. In the 1960's the Faslane base was transformed and re-built ashore to accommodate our Polaris force of strategic missile firing submarines together with nuclear powered fleet submarines and a squadron of the conventional Porpoise and Oberon class. Gosport has grown as a training school for the ever increasingly important submarine arm and a squadron of conventional submarines continue to be operated from there. A shore based nuclear/conventional submarine base has been built at Devonport and nuclear submarine base refitting facilities have been developed at Chatham and Rosyth. The submarine service has increased in size from some 3000 officers and men to over 8000 manning ever more complex vessels requiring far greater technical skills than were possessed by those of us afloat at the end of the war.

Despite all these technical advances our submarines have lagged behind in their weapons. For all too long the pre World War II Mk 8 torpedo has been it's main armament. Happily the Mk 8 has at last been replaced by the Tigerfish and other high performance torpedoes. Nevertheless the submarine, and in particular the nuclear powered fleet submarine of to-day, will not reach it's true potential weapon of war until it has been equipped with tactical anti-ship missiles which can be fired from outside the sonar defences of a surface force. "The demand for a long range weapon has been accelerated by the effectiveness of close range anti-submarine defence. There is a clear need for such a weapon if we are to counter the formidable force of powerful missile armed ships in the Soviet fleet. The addition of such a weapon to our fleet submarine armoury will add versatility to it's flexibility and effectiveness and will provide a powerful maritime strike capability" — all the more important now with the passing of the Navy's strike aircraft carriers. Thus I wrote in that well known naval reference book — Jane's Fighting Ships — nearly ten years ago. It remains even truer to-day.

John Roxburgh

Hindhead, Surrey
May 1981.

3

Submarines

'U' CLASS

Built to replace the 'H' boats, the 'U' Class, their simple design was intended to make them suitable only for anti-submarine training. In that role, they would not need to be armed, but this idea was soon changed to make them able to undertake war patrols. The pre-war vessels were fitted with external and internal torpedo tubes. During war-time construction though, the external tubes were omitted.

Twenty one of these submarines became war losses, one of which — "UNTAMED" was salvaged, refitted and re-named "VITALITY".

Three of the Class — UNBROKEN, UNISON and URSULA — were loaned to the Soviet Navy; Two — UNTIRING and UPSTART — to the Royal Hellenic Navy; Two — P47 and VARNE — to the Royal Netherlands Navy; Two — P52 and URCHIN — to the Polish Navy; and VOX to France.

Ship	Launch Date	Builder
UNA	10 June 1941	H.M. Dockyard, Chatham
UPRIGHT	21 April 1940	Vickers Armstrong, Barrow
URCHIN	30 Sept. 1940	Vickers Armstrong, Barrow
URSULA	16 Feb. 1938	Vickers Armstrong, Barrow

Displacement (tons) 540 (surfaced); 730 (submerged) **Length** 191 ft. **Beam** 16 ft. **Draught** 12 ft. 9 ins. **Speed (knots)** 11¾ (surfaced); 8 (submerged) **Armament** one 12 PDR A.A. or 3" A.A. **Torpedo Tubes** six torpedo tubes (all forward) — four in "UNA" and "URCHIN", ten torpedoes (eight in "UNA" and "URCHIN") **Complement** 33.

War Losses

UMPIRE (1941); UNBEATEN (1942); UNDAUNTED (1941); UNDINE (1940); UNION (1941); UNIQUE (1942); UNITY (1940); UPHOLDER (1942); URGE (1942); USK (1941); UTMOST (1941).

Submarines

Notes

UNA

11 April 1949   —   Sold to E. Rees Shipbreaking Co. Ltd., of Llanelly.

UPRIGHT

19 Dec. 1945   —   Sold to the West of Scotland Shipbreaking Co.

March 1946   —   Arrived Troon to be broken up.

URCHIN

11 Jan. 1941   —   Loaned to the Polish Navy; re-named "SOKOL".

1946   —   Returned to Royal Navy and renamed P97.

1949   —   Broken up.

URSULA

1944-49   —   Loaned to the Soviet Navy, as V4.

May 1950   —   Sold to Brechin of Grangemouth.

P52 (as R. Danish N. Springeren) July 1952

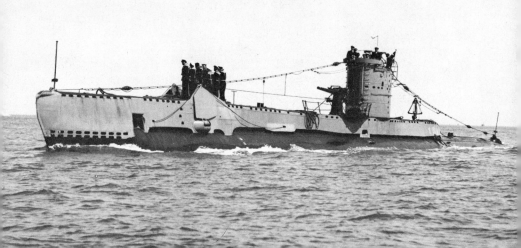

Submarines

'U' CLASS — SECOND GROUP

Ship	Launch Date	Builder
P47	27 July 1942	Vickers Armstrong, Barrow
P52	11 Oct. 1942	Vickers Armstrong, Barrow
ULLESWATER	27 Nov. 1940	Vickers Armstrong, Barrow
ULTIMATUM	11 Feb. 1941	Vickers Armstrong, Barrow
ULTOR	12 Oct. 1942	Vickers Armstrong, Barrow
UMBRA	15 March 1941	Vickers Armstrong, Barrow
UNBENDING	12 May 1941	Vickers Armstrong, Barrow
UNBROKEN	4 Nov. 1941	Vickers Armstrong, Barrow
UNISON	5 Nov. 1941	Vickers Armstrong, Barrow
UNITED	18 Dec. 1941	Vickers Armstrong, Barrow
UNIVERSAL	10 Nov. 1942	Vickers Armstrong, Tyne
UNRIVALLED	16 Feb. 1942	Vickers Armstrong, Barrow
UNRUFFLED	19 Dec. 1941	Vickers Armstrong, Barrow
UNRULY	28 July 1942	Vickers Armstrong, Barrow
UNSEEN	16 April 1942	Vickers Armstrong, Barrow
UNSHAKEN	17 Feb. 1942	Vickers Armstrong, Barrow
UNSPARING	28 July 1943	Vickers Armstrong, Tyne
UNSWERVING	19 July 1943	Vickers Armstrong, Tyne
UNTAMED	8 Dec. 1942	Vickers Armstrong, Tyne
UNTIRING	20 Jan. 1943	Vickers Armstrong, Tyne
UPROAR	27 Nov. 1940	Vickers Armstrong, Barrow
UPSTART	24 Nov. 1942	Vickers Armstrong, Barrow
UTHER	6 April 1943	Vickers Armstrong, Tyne
VARANGIAN	4 April 1943	Vickers Armstrong, Tyne
VARNE (i)	22 Jan. 1943	Vickers Armstrong, Barrow
VOX (i)	23 Jan. 1943	Vickers Armstrong, Barrow

Displacement (tons) 545 (surfaced); 735 (submerged) **Length** 196 ft. 9 ins **Beam** 16 ft. **Draught** 12 ft. 9 ins. **Speed (knots)** 11¾ (surfaced); 8 (submerged) **Torpedo Tubes** six 21″ (all forward), ten torpedoes **Complement** 33.

Submarines

War Losses

P32 (1941); P33 (1941); P38 (1942); P41 (1943); P48 (1942).

P36 was sunk in Sliema Harbour, Malta in 1942; was salvaged on 7 August 1958; and scuttled off Malta on 22 August 1958.

P39 — was sunk at Malta in 1942; was salvaged and beached in June 1943. Broken up in 1954.

USURPER (1943).

UNTAMED — foundered in the Firth of Clyde on 30 May 1943; was raised on 5 July 1943; refitted and re-named "VITALITY". Was sold on 13 February 1946, arriving Troon in March to be broken up.

VANDAL — wrecked in Firth of Clyde 24 February 1943.

Cancelled Orders

P81-P87 (inclusive).

Notes

P47

1942	—	Loaned to Royal Netherlands Navy. Re-named "DOLFIJN".
1947	—	Returned to Royal Navy and broken up.

P52

1942	—	Loaned to Polish Navy. Re-named 'DZIK'.
1946	—	Transferred to Royal Danish Navy, becoming 'U.I.'
1948	—	Re-named 'SPRINGEREN'.
April 1958	—	Sold to Metal Industries. Arrived Faslane to be broken up.

ULLESWATER

Feb. 1943	—	Named 'ULLESWATER'.
April 1943	—	Re-named 'UPROAR'. (See "UPROAR".)

ULTIMATUM

23 Dec. 1949	—	Sold to Smith and Houston.
Feb. 1950	—	Arrived Port Glasgow to be broken up.

Submarines

Notes

ULTOR

22 Jan. 1946   —   Sold to T.W. Ward Ltd. and arrived Briton Ferry to be broken up.

UMBRA

9 July 1946   —   Sold to Hughes Bolckow of Blyth to be broken up.

UNBENDING

23 Dec. 1949   —   Sold to C.W. Dorkin.

May 1950   —   Arrived Gateshead to be broken up.

UNBROKEN

1944-49   —   Along with UNISON and ROYAL SOVEREIGN was on loan to Soviet Navy (as V2).

9 May 1950   —   Sold to J.J. King & arrived Gateshead to be broken up.

UNISON

1944-49   —   Along with UNBROKEN and ROYAL SOVEREIGN was on loan to Soviet Navy (as V3).

19 May 1950   —   Sold to Stockton Shipbreaking & Salvage Co. & arrived Stockton-on-Tees to be broken up.

UNITED

12 Feb. 1946   —   Sold to West of Scotland Shipbreaking Co. & arrived Troon to be broken up.

UNIVERSAL

Feb. 1946   —   Sold to J. Cashmore but . . .

June 1946   —   Broken up by T.W. Ward at Milford Haven.

Submarines

Notes

UNRIVALLED

22 Jan. 1946   —   Sold to T.W. Ward & arrived Briton Ferry to be broken up.

UNRUFFLED

Jan. 1946   —   Broken up at Troon.

UNRULY

Feb. 1946   —   Sold to T.W. Ward & arrived Inverkeithing to be broken up.

UNSEEN

Sept. 1949   —   Sold to T.W. Ward & arrived Hayle, Cornwall to be broken up.

HMS Untiring (November 1954)

Submarines

Notes

UNSHAKEN

March 1946 — Sold to West of Scotland Shipbreaking Co. & arrived Troon to be broken up.

UNSPARING

14 Feb. 1946 — Sold to T.W. Ward & arrived Inverkeithing to be broken up.

UNSWERVING

10 July 1949 — Sold to J. Cashmore & arrived Newport to be broken up.

UNTAMED

Details under ''War Losses''.

HMS Upstart (June 1954)

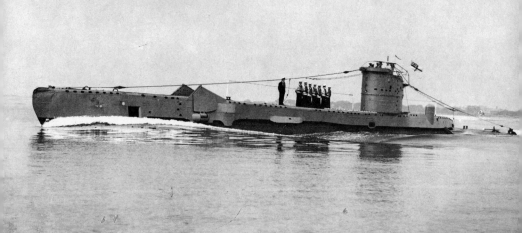

Submarines

UNTIRING

1945-52   —   Loaned to Royal Hellenic Navy — re-named "ZIFIAS".

25 July 1957   —   Expended as an A/S target off Start Point.

UPROAR

See also "ULLESWATER".

13 Feb. 1946   —   Sold to T.W. Ward, Inverkeithing.

UPSTART

1945-52   —   Loaned to Royal Hellenic Navy. Re-named "AMFITRITE".

29 July 1957   —   Expended as an A/S target off the Isle of Wight.

UTHER

Feb. 1950   —   Sold to T.W. Ward. Arrived Hayle, Cornwall to be broken up.

VARANGIAN

June 1949   —   Sold to J.J. King of Gateshead, to be broken up.

VARNE (i)

28 March 1943   —   Transferred to the Royal Norwegian Navy. Re-named "ULA".

Dec. 1965   —   Sold to H. Eckhardt Gmbh (Hamburg), for breaking up.

VOX

1943-1946   —   Loaned to the French Navy. Re-named "CURIE".

July 1946   —   Returned to Royal Navy and named P67.

2 May 1949   —   Sold to T.W. Ward & arrived Milford Haven to be broken up.

Submarines

'V' CLASS

These boats were a modification of the 'U' design, but being of partly welded construction they were able to dive deeper. Construction was much reduced when the war in the Mediterranean eased off, and stopped altogether when VE-Day arrived.

Twenty of this Class were cancelled:- ULEX, UNBRIDLED, UPAS, UPWARD, UTOPIA, VANTAGE, VEHEMENT, VENOM, VERVE, VETO, VIRILE, VISITANT, and eight un-named vessels.

Four — VARIANCE, VENTURER, VIKING, VOTARY — were loaned to Royal Norwegian Navy; Four — VELDT, VENGEFUL, VIRULENT, VOLATILE, — to Royal Hellenic Navy; Two to French Navy — VINEYARD and VORTEX; and one — VULPINE — to Royal Danish Navy.

Ship	Launch Date	Builder
UPSHOT	24 Feb. 1944	Vickers Armstrong, Barrow
URTICA	23 March 1944	Vickers Armstrong, Barrow
VAGABOND	19 Sept. 1944	Vickers Armstrong, Tyne
VAMPIRE	20 July 1943	Vickers Armstrong, Barrow
VARIANCE	22 May 1944	Vickers Armstrong, Barrow
VARNE (ii)	24 Feb. 1944	Vickers Armstrong, Tyne
VELDT	19 July 1943	Vickers Armstrong, Barrow
VENGEFUL	20 July 1944	Vickers Armstrong, Barrow
VENTURER	4 May 1943	Vickers Armstrong, Barrow
VIGOROUS	15 Oct. 1943	Vickers Armstrong, Barrow
VIKING	5 May 1943	Vickers Armstrong, Barrow
VINEYARD	8 May 1944	Vickers Armstrong, Barrow
VIRTUE	29 Nov. 1943	Vickers Armstrong, Barrow
VIRULENT	23 May 1944	Vickers Armstrong, Tyne
VISIGOTH	30 Nov. 1943	Vickers Armstrong, Barrow
VIVID	15 Sept. 1943	Vickers Armstrong, Tyne
VOLATILE	20 June 1944	Vickers Armstrong, Tyne
VORACIOUS	11 Nov. 1943	Vickers Armstrong, Tyne
VORTEX	19 Aug. 1944	Vickers Armstrong, Barrow

Submarines

Ship	Launch Date	Builder
VOTARY	21 Aug. 1944	Vickers Armstrong, Tyne
VOX (ii)	28 Sept. 1943	Vickers Armstrong, Barrow
VULPINE	28 Dec. 1943	Vickers Armstrong, Tyne

Displacement (tons) 545 (surfaced); 740 (submerged) **Length** 204 ft. 6 ins. **Beam** 16 ft. **Draught** 12 ft. 9 ins. **Speed (knots)** 12¾ (surfaced); 8 (submerged) **Armament** one 3″ A.A., three .303″ **Torpedo Tubes** four 21″ (all forward), eight torpedoes **Complement** 37.

Notes

UPSHOT

22 Nov. 1948 — Sold to T.W. Ward & arrived Preston to be broken up.

URTICA

March 1950 — Sold to T.. Ward & arrived Milford Haven to be broken up.

VAGABOND

26 Jan. 1950 — Sold to J. Cashmore & arrived Newport to be broken up.

VAMPIRE

5 March 1950 — Sold to J.J. King & arrived Gateshead to be broken up.

VARIANCE

1944 — Transferred to Royal Norweigian Navy. Re-named "UTSIRA".

Dec. 1965 — Sold to Eckhardt Gmbh. Arrived Hamburg to be broken up.

Submarines

Notes

VARNE (ii)

Sept. 1958 — Sold to West of Scotland Shipbreaking Co. & arrived Troon to be broken up.

VELDT

1943 — Lent to Royal Hellenic Navy. Re-named "PIPINOS".

10 Dec. 1957 — Returned to Royal Navy. Broken up by Clayton and Davie Ltd. at Dunston-on-Tyne.

VENGEFUL

1945-57 — Lent to Royal Hellenic Navy. Re-named "DELPHIN".

22 March 1958 — Sold to J.J. King of Gateshead. Arrived to be broken up.

HMS Venturer (as R. Nor. N. Utstein) June 1951

Submarines

VENTURER

Aug. 1946 — Transferred to Royal Norwegian Navy at Rothesay. Re-named "UTSTEIN".

1965 — Sold to Sarpsborg Shipbreakers.

VIGOROUS

23 Dec. 1949 — Sold to Stockton Shipping & Salvage Co. Broken up at Stockton-on-Tees.

VIKING

Aug. 1946 — Sold to Royal Norwegian Navy. Re-named "UTVAER".

1965 — Sold to Sarpsborg Shipbreakers.

VINEYARD

1944-47 — Lent to French Navy. Re-named 'DORIS'.

June 1950 — Sold to Metal Industries. Arrived Charlestown, Fife, to be broken up.

VIRTUE

19 May 1946 — Arrived Cochin, India, to be broken up.

VIRULENT

29 May 1946 — Lent to Royal Hellenic Navy. Re-named "ARGONAFTIS".

3 Oct. 1958 — Returned to Royal Navy.

15 Dec. 1958 — During tow from Malta to the Tyne she broke adrift.

6 Jan. 1959 — Was towed in to Pasajes by fishing boats.

1961 — Sold at Pasajes to Spanish Shipbreakers.

April 1961 — Broken up.

Submarines

VISIGOTH

March 1949	—	Sold to T.W. Ward.
April 1950	—	Arrived Hayle, Cornwall, to be broken up.

VIVID

Oct. 1950 — Sold to Shipbreaking Industries. Arrived Faslane to be broken up.

VOLATILE

1946-1958 — Lent to Royal Hellenic Navy. Re-named "TRIANA". On return was sold to Clayton and Davie.

23 Dec. 1958 — Arrived at Dunston-on-Tyne, to be broken up.

VORACIOUS

19 May 1946 — Arrived Cochin, India, to be broken up.

VORTEX

1944-47 — Lent to the French Navy (re-named "MORSE").

1947-Jan.'58 — Lent to the Royal Danish Navy (re-named "SAELEN").

Aug. 1958 — Arrived Faslane to be broken up by Metal Industries.

VOTARY

July 1946 — Transferred to the Royal Norwegian Navy. Re-named "UTHAUG".

1966 — Broken up in Grimstad.

VOX (ii)

1943 — Replaced VOX (i) — a 'U' class boat loaned to France.

19 May 1946 — Arrived Cochin, India, to be broken up.

Submarines

Notes

VULPINE

Sept. 1947-1958 —	Lent to the Royal Danish Navy. (Re-named "STOREN").
June 1959 —	Sold to Shipbreaking Industries and arrived Faslane to be broken up.

HMS Vulpine (as R. Danish N. Storen) Feb 1958

HMS Varne (as R. Nor N. Ula) July 1949

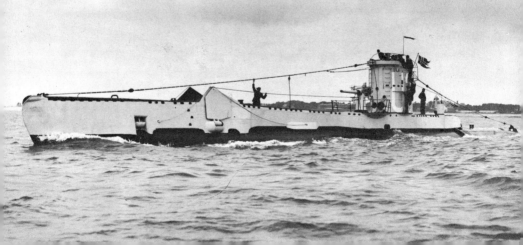

Submarines

'S' CLASS

These boats were based on an improved 'H' Class design but with an increased speed and improved endurance to provide a larger radius of operations. They were extremely manoeuvrable and could dive in under 30 seconds.

The first group had their 3″ guns sited on a forward extension of the conning tower, but the second group's gun was mounted on the submarine's casing. In the later boats, for service in the Far East theatre of war, the 3″ gun was replaced by a 4″. The boats built during the war were partly or, in later production, wholly of welded construction.

To further extend their range of operations, the boats sent to the Far East had some of their ballast tanks converted into oil fuel tanks. This increase in oil fuel stowage was, however, specifically built in to the third group of boats.

A large number of this class were still in service at the end of World War 2. Many with long active service were soon sold for breaking up and others expended as targets. Several were transferred, loaned or sold to foreign navies — 1 to the Royal Netherlands Navy, Three to Portugal, Four to France, and Two to Israel.

"SEA DEVIL" was the last boat of this class to be used for operational purposes.

'S' CLASS — FIRST GROUP

Ship	Launch Date	Builder
STURGEON	8 Jan. 1932	H.M. Dockyard, Chatham

Displacement (tons) 640 (surfaced); 935 (submerged); **Length** 202 ft. 6 ins. **Beam** 24 ft. **Draught** 10 ft. 6 ins. **Speed (knots)** 13 ¾ (surfaced); 8 (submerged) **Armament** one 3″ A.A. gun; one .303″ **Torpedo Tubes** six 21″ (all forward) twelve torpedoes **Complement** 36.

Submarines

Notes

STURGEON

1943-45	—	Transferred to Royal Netherlands Navy, as "ZEEHOND."
Jan. 1947	—	Arrived at Granton Shipbreakers to be broken up.

War Losses

SEAHORSE (1940); STARFISH (1940); SWORDFISH (1940);

"S" CLASS — SECOND GROUP

Ship	Launch Date	Builder
SEA WOLF	28 Nov. 1935	Scotts, — Greenock.

Displacement (tons) 670 (surfaced); 960 (submerged); **Length** 208 ft. 9 ins. **Beam** 24 ft. **Draught** 10 ft. 6 ins. **Speed (knots)** 13¾ (surfaced); 8 (submerged) **Armament** one 3″ gun; one .303″ **Torpedo Tubes** six 21″ (all forward) twelve torpedoes **Complement** 39.

Notes

Nov. 1945	—	Sold to Marine Industries at Montreal, to be broken up.

War Losses

SALMON (1940); SHARK (1940); SNAPPER (1941); SPEARFISH (1940); STERLET (1940); SUNFISH (lost after transfer to the Soviet Navy (1944).

Expended as a Target

SEALION. Expended as an A/S target off the Isle of Arran on 3 March 1945.

Submarines

"S" CLASS — THIRD GROUP

Ship	Launch Date	Builder
SAFARI	18 Nov. 1941	Cammell Laird, Birkenhead
SAGA	14 March 1945	Cammell Laird, Birkenhead
SANGUINE	15 Feb. 1945	Cammell Laird, Birkenhead
SATYR	28 Sept. 1942	Scotts — Greenock.
SCEPTRE	9 Jan. 1943	Scotts — Greenock.
SCORCHER	18 Dec. 1944	Cammell Laird, Birkenhead
SCOTSMAN	18 Aug. 1944	Scotts — Greenock
SCYTHIAN	14 Apr. 1944	Scotts — Greenock
SEA DEVIL	30 Jan. 1945	Scotts — Greenock
SEA DOG	11 June 1942	Cammell Laird, Birkenhead
SEA NYMPH	29 July 1942	Cammell Laird, Birkenhead
SEA ROVER	8 Feb. 1943	Launched-Scotts of Greenock
		Completed-Vickers Armstrong, Barrow
SEA SCOUT	24 march 1944	Cammell Laird, Birkenhead
SELENE	24 April 1944	Cammell Laird, Birkenhead
SENESCHAL	23 April 1945	Scotts — Greenock
SENTINEL	27 July 1945	Scotts — Greenock
SERAPH	25 Oct. 1941	Vickers Armstrong, Barrow
SHAKESPEARE	8 Dec. 1941	Vickers Armstrong, Barrow
SHALIMAR	22 April 1943	H.M. Dockyard, Chatham
SIBYL	29 April 1942	Cammell Laird, Birkenhead
SIDON	4 Sept 1944	Cammell Laird, Birkenhead
SIRDAR	26 March 1943	Launched-Scotts - Greenock
		Completed-Vickers Armstrong, Barrow
SLEUTH	6 July 1944	Cammell Laird, Birkenhead
SOLENT	8 June 1944	Cammell Laird, Birkenhead
SPARK	28 Dec. 1943	Scotts — Greenock

Submarines

Ship	Launch Date	Builder
SPEARHEAD	2 Oct. 1944	Cammell Laird, Birkenhead
SPIRIT	20 July 1943	Cammell Laird, Birkenhead
SPITEFUL	5 June 1943	Scotts — Greenock
SPORTSMAN	17 April 1942	H.M. Dockyard, Chatham
SPRINGER	14 May 1945	Cammell Laird, Birkenhead
SPUR	17 Nov. 1944	Cammell Laird, Birkenhead
STATESMAN	14 Sept. 1943	Cammell Laird, Birkenhead
STOIC	9 April 1943	Cammell Laird, Birkenhead
STORM	18 May 1943	Cammell Laird, Birkenhead
STRONGBOW	30 Aug. 1943	Scotts — Greenock
STURDY	30 Sept. 1943	Cammell Laird, Birkenhead
STYGIAN	30 Nov. 1943	Cammell Laird, Birkenhead
SUBTLE	27 Jan. 1944	Cammell Laird, Birkenhead
SUPREME	24 Feb. 1944	Cammell Laird, Birkenhead
SURF	10 Dec. 1942	Cammell Laird, Birkenhead

Displacement (tons) 715 (surfaced); 990 (submerged); **Length** 217 ft. **Beam** 23 ft. 6 ins. **Draught** 11ft. **Speed (knots)** 14¾ (surfaced); 8 (submerged) **Armament** one 3″ gun (4″ in later boats; one 20 mm A.A., three .303″ **Torpedo Tubes** seven 21″, (six forward and one aft), thirteen torpedoes **Complement** 48.

War Losses

P222 (Ex-P72) 1942; SAHIB 1943; SARACEN 1943; SICKLE 1944; SIMOOM 1943; SPLENDID 1943; STONEHENGE 1944; STRATEGEM 1944; SYRTIS 1944.

Cancelled Orders

SEA ROBIN; SPRIGHTLY; SURFACE; SURGE.

Expended as a Target

STUBBORN — Expended as an A/S target off Malta on 30 April, 1946.

Submarines

SAFARI

7 Jan. 1946	—	Sold to J. Cashmore Ltd., Newport, but was wrecked the next day whilst being towed to the shipbreakers.

SAGA

11 Oct. 1948	—	Transferred to the Portuguese Navy at Gosport and re-named NAULTILO.
1969	—	On Disposal list.

SANGUINE

Oct. 1958	—	Sold to he Israeli Navy & re-named RAHAV.
May 1960	—	Delivered to Israel.
1969	—	Broken up at Haifa.

SATYR

1952	—	Transferred to the French Navy, & re-named SAPHIR. Returned to the R.N. 1961.
11 Aug. 1961	—	Arrived Rosyth, and sold to Shipbreaking Industries Ltd.
4 April 1962	—	Arrived at Charlestown, Fife, to be broken up.

SCEPTRE

Sept. 1949	—	Sold to J.J. King, of Gateshead, to be broken up.

SCORCHER

14 Sept. 1962	—	Sold to Shipbreaking Industries & arrived Charlestown, Fife, to be broken up.

Submarines

Notes

SCOTSMAN

1961	—	Laid up in reserve in the Gareloch. Sold to West of Scotland Shipbreaking Co.
19 Nov. 1964	—	Arrived at Troon to be broken up (see additional notes).

SCYTHIAN

8 Aug. 1960	—	Sold to Shipbreaking Industries & arrived Charlestown, Fife, to be broken up.

SEA DEVIL

4 June 1962	—	The last operational submarine of this class at sea. Returned to Portsmouth after service in the Mediterranean, to pay off for disposal. Sold to Metal Recoveries.
15 Dec. 1965	—	Towed from Portsmouth to Newhaven, where she was broken up.

HMS Sanguine (September 1947)

Submarines

SEA DOG

Aug. 1948   —   Arrived Troon to be broken after being sold to West of Scotland Shipbreaking Co.

SEA NYMPH

June 1948   —   Sold to West of Scotland Shipbreaking Co. & arrived Troon to be broken up.

SEA ROVER

Oct. 1949   —   Sold to Metal Industries, and broken up at Faslane.

SEA SCOUT

Aug. 1962   —   Paid off at Gosport for Disposal. Sold to T.W. Ward Ltd.

14 Dec. 1965   —   Towed from Portsmouth, along with SERAPH to be broken up at Briton Ferry.

SELENE

6 June 1961   —   Sold to J.J. King Ltd. & arrived Gateshead to be broken up.

SENESCHAL

23 Aug. 1960   —   Sold to Clayton and Davie, Ltd. & arrived Dunston-on-Tyne to be broken up.

SENTINEL

28 Feb. 1962   —   Sold to Lynch of Rochester. Broken up at Gillingham.

HMS Sea Devil

HMS Sea Scout (June 1948)

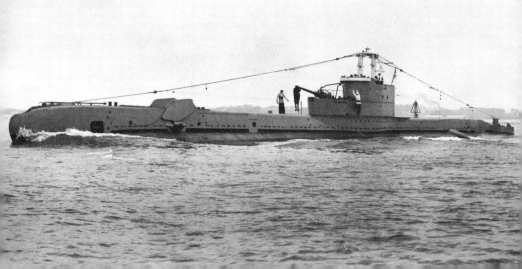

Submarines

Notes

SERAPH

1965	—	Sold to T.W. Ward Ltd.
14 Dec. 1965	—	Towed, with SEA SCOUT, from Portsmouth. She broke from tow and was adrift for 24 hours on 15 Dec.
20 Dec. 1965	—	Arrived Briton Ferry, Swansea, to be broken up.

SHAKESPEARE

3 Jan. 1945	—	Bombed by Japanese aircraft in the Nankaun Strait; was written off as a constructive loss.
14 July 1946	—	Sold to T.W. Ward Ltd. of Briton Ferry, Swansea, and broken up.

SHALIMAR

July 1950	—	Sold to West of Scotland Shipbreaking Co. Arrived Troon to be broken up.

SIBYL

March 1948	—	Sold to West of Scotland Shipbreaking Co. Arrived Troon to be broken up.

SIDON

16 June 1955	—	Sank after torpedo explosion on board, in Portland Harbour. Salvaged a week later (see additional notes).
14 June 1957	—	Was towed out of Portland and sunk for use as an A/S target on the sea bed.

SIRDAR

1959	—	Used in experiments at Rosyth by the Naval Construction Research Establishment.
31 May 1965	—	Sold to P.& W. McLellan & arrived Boness to be broken up.

Submarines

Notes

SLEUTH
15 Sept. 1958   —   Sold to Shipbreaking Industries & arrived
                      Charlestown, Fife, to be broken up.

SOLENT
28 Aug. 1961   —   Sold to West of Scotland Shipbreaking Co.
                     & arrived Troon to be broken up.

SPARK
28 Oct. 1949   —   Sold to Metal Industries, Faslane to be
                     broken up.

SPEARHEAD
1948   —   Sold to Portuguese Navy. Re-named
                     NEPTUNO.
1967   —   On the Disposal list.

HMS Solent (July 1951)

Submarines

Notes

SPIRIT
4 July 1950   —   Sold to T.W. Ward Ltd & arrived Grays, Essex, to be broken up.

SPITEFUL
1952   —   Transferred to the French Navy. Re-named SIRENE.
24 Oct. 1958   —   Returned to R.N.
9 July 1963   —   Sold to Metal Industries. Towed from Portsmouth.
15 July 1963   —   Arrived Faslane to be broken up.

SPORTSMAN
1951   —   Transferred to the French Navy. Renamed SIBYLLE.
23 Sept. 1952   —   Foundered off Toulon. (See additional notes).

SPRINGER
Oct. 1958   —   Sold to Israeli Navy (for £200,000). Re-named TANIN (meaning Crocodile).
9 Oct. 1958   —   Handed over at Gosport. Sailed to Mersey for refit by Cammell Laird.
Dec. 1959   —   Delivered to Israel.
1972   —   On Disposal list.

SPUR
1948   —   Sold to the Portuguese Navy. Re-named NARVAL.
1969   —   De-commissioned.

STATESMAN
1952   —   Transferred to the French Navy. Re-named SULTANE.
5 Nov. 1959   —   Returned to the R.N.
3 Jan. 1961   —   Sold to H.G. Pounds, of Portsmouth, and broken up.

Submarines

Notes

STOIC
July 1950   —   Sold to W.H. Arnott Young, Dalmuir, for breaking up (see additional notes).

STORM
Sept. 1949   —   Sold to West of Scotland Shipbreaking Co. & arrived Troon to be broken up.

STRONGBOW
April 1946   —   Sold to T.W. Ward Ltd. & arrived Preston, to be broken up.

STURDY
July 1957   —   Sold in Malta.
9 May 1958   —   Arrived Dunston-on-Tyne, to be broken up by Clayton and Davie, Ltd.

STYGIAN
28 Oct. 1949   —   Sold to Metal Industries. Arrived Faslane to be broken up.

SUBTLE
June 1959   —   Sold Shipbreaking Industries & arrived Charlestown, Fife, to be broken up.

SUPREME
July 1950   —   Sold to West of Scotland Shipbreaking Co. & arrived Troon to be broken up.

SURF
28 Oct. 1949   —   Sold to Metal Industries & arrived Faslane to be broken up.

Submarines

Additional Notes

SCOTSMAN

Was deliberately sunk in Kames Bay, Bute, in the spring of 1964 so that fresh experience could be gained with the two lifting craft stationed on the Clyde, which had not been used since the Suez crisis. She was then salvaged in June 1964 and sold to the West of Scotland Shipbreaking Company.

SCEPTRE

On the 8 August 1949 she was damaged by an explosion and became partially flooded and filled with chlorine gas. She was suspended on salvage wires in over 500 feet of water and was in danger of sinking if she became completely flooded. One of her ship's company, L.E.M. C.C. Anderson, volunteered to enter the submarine. Fully aware of the danger he was facing, he managed to reach the pump room, connect the main ballast pump thereby giving the submarine sufficient buoyancy to float her. His courage and skill undoubtedly saved the submarine.

SERAPH

Whilst awaiting disposal at Portsmouth in 1963 various "souvenirs", including one periscope and other fittings, were removed from her for incorporation in a monument to be erected at the Military College of South Carolina, U.S.A. Dedicated in November 1963, the monument was built to commemorate Anglo-American co-operation in World War 2 submarine operations.

It was considered this co-operation was best symbolised by "SERAPH" which had once been commanded by a British and an American Captain. It was "SERAPH" that landed U.S. General Mark Clark and other high ranking officers in North Africa on an Intelligence mission. The submarine became U.S.S. SERAPH for a few days.

In April 1943 "SERAPH" put the body of "The Man Who Never Was" ashore on the Spanish coast. The body, with faked documents and dressed as a Royal Marine officer, tricked the Germans into believing the allies had other plans — apart from the invasion of Sicily.

HMS Scotsman

HMS Seraph (June 1962)

Submarines

Additional Notes

SIDON

At 0825 on the 16 June 1955, SIDON was lying alongside the depot ship MAIDSTONE at Portland when one of her torpedoes exploded. The torpedoes had no warheads, but did have the new volatile hydrogen peroxide propellant. The crew had just embarked the torpedoes before going to sea for trial firings.

A sudden uprush of air and smoke poured through the conning tower hatch. Her Captain and others who were on the bridge, and others from MAIDSTONE entered the submarine to assist rescue operations. At 0845 the submarine sank without warning by the bows. There were 56 men on board at the time — crew, trainees and trials personnel for the trip to sea. Three officers and ten ratings lost their lives but the remainder were saved.

The wreck was raised on the 23 June 1955, and beached the next day. The 13 bodies were recovered on the 25th.

SPORTSMAN

As the French submarine "SIBYLLE", on 23 September 1952, she disappeared in the Mediterranean 38 miles east of Toulon. She was diving between Cannes and the island of Porquerolles. The cause of the disaster, which cost 47 lives, is still unknown.

STOIC

In 1948 a large fleet, comprising two lifting craft of 1200 tons lift capacity, the coastal salvage vessel "SUCCOUR", boom defence vessel "BARILLA", a floating science laboratory, two tugs "JAUNTY" and "SAUCY", two M.F.V.'s, and H.M.S. FLAMBOROUGH HEAD, assembled at Kyle in Scotland to carry out deep diving trials on the submarine "STOIC".

Eighteen miles north of Kyle in the Inner Sound, between the mainland of Rosshire and Islands of Raasay and South Rona, the "STOIC" was lowered into what is the deepest 'hole' anywhere round the British Isles. The "STOIC" eventually crushed and flooded over 200 feet below her safe diving depth — exactly as predicted by the experts. She was hauled up on a beach and sold for breaking up by Arnott Young of Dalmuir, in July 1950.

"SUPREME" and "VARNE" were also used in similar tests.

HMS Sidon (June 1953)

HMS Sportsman (August 1947)

Submarines

'T' CLASS

This class of patrol type submarines of saddle tank design gave good service during World War 2, but suffered heavy casualties — 16 of them being lost. For a period after the end of the war, along with the 'A' class, they formed the mainstay of our underwater forces. All were eventually fitted with "Snort" equipment.

In the first group all the torpedo tubes were positioned to fire forwards but later vessels had an external tube added and two tubes amidships turned to fire astern.

The early built boats were of rivetted construction but as the numbers increased so did the use of welding methods. This was to affect the varied modifications carried out on this class between 1951-1956.

The rivetted hull boats — TALENT, TAPIR, TEREDO, TIRELESS, TOKEN, THULE & TUDOR — were modernised by being "streamlined". The bridge was converted into a fin, housing periscopes, radar masts, etc., and all guns and external torpedo tubes removed to improve underwater speed — without any increase in engine power — and to make them quieter running.

The welded hull boats were "stretched" having from 12 to 20 feet added amidships. This enabled them to have extra batteries and diesel electric propulsion fitted. TABARD, TIPTOE, TRUMP and TRUNCHEON had 20 feet added; TACITURN 14 feet; THERMOPYLAE, TOTEM and TURPIN 12 feet. The pressure hull was severed at the engine room section, the two halves moved apart and a new section built in. The periscopes and aerials were enclosed in a fin and again all guns and external torpedo tubes were removed.

The last 'T' class submarine used for sea service was TIPTOE, who celebrated her 25th birthday with a visit to her "birthplace" at Barrow-in-Furness.

Submarines

"T" CLASS —FIRST GROUP

Ship	Launch Date	Builder
TAKU	20 May 1939	Cammell Laird, Birkenhead
TORBAY	9 April 1940	H.M. Dockyard, Chatham
TRIBUNE	8 Dec. 1938	Scotts, Greenock
TRIDENT	7 Dec. 1938	Cammell Laird, Birkenhead
TRUANT	5 May 1939	Vickers Armstrong, Barrow
TUNA	10 May 1940	Scotts, Greenock

Displacement (**tons**) 1,090 (surfaced); 1,573 (submerged); **Length** 275 ft. **Beam** 26 ft. 6 ins. **Draught** 12 ft. **Speed** (**knots**) 15¼ (surfaced); 8 (submerged) **Armament** one 4″ gun, three .303″. **Torpedo Tubes** ten 21″ (eight forward and two amidships), sixteen torpedoes **Complement** 56.

Notes

TAKU
Nov. 1946   —   Sold to E. Rees, Llanelly, and broken up.

TORBAY
19 Dec. 1945   —   Sold to T.W. Ward Ltd., Briton Ferry for breaking up.

TRIBUNE
July 1947   —   Sold to Milford Haven Dry Dock Co. and arrived Milford Haven. Breaking up commenced two months later.

TRIDENT
17 Feb. 1946   —   Sold to J. Cashmore and arrived Newport for breaking up.

Submarines

Notes

TRUANT

19 Dec. 1945	—	Sold to T.W. Ward, Briton Ferry.
9 Dec. 1946	—	In a gale, she parted her tow en route to the breakers, eventually ending up on the rocks at Cherbourg.

TUNA

24 June 1946	—	Sold to T.W. Ward. Arrived Briton Ferry for breaking up.

War Losses

TALISMAN (1942); TARPON (1940); TETRARCH (1941); THE-TIS (foundered in 1939); salvaged, but lost — as the THUNDER-BOLT — in 1943); THISTLE (1940); TIGRIS (1943); TRIAD (1940) TRITON (1940); TRIUMPH (1942).

"T" CLASS — SECOND GROUP

Ship	Launch Date	Builder
THRASHER	28 Nov. 1940	Cammell Laird, Birkenhead
TRUSTY	14 March 1941	Vickers Armstrong, Barrow

Displacement (**tons**) 1,090 (surfaced); 1,571 (submerged) **Length** 273 ft. 6 ins. **Beam** 26 ft. 6 ins. **Draught** 12 ft. **Speed** (**knots**) 15¼ (surfaced); 8 (submerged) **Armament** one 4" gun, three .303" **Torpedo Tubes** eleven 21" (eight forward, two midships and one aft), seventeen torpedoes **Complement** 61.

Submarines

Notes

THRASHER

9 March 1947	—	Sold to T.W. Ward. Arrived Briton Ferry to be broken up.

TRUSTY

July 1947	—	Sold Milford Haven Dry Dock Co. Arrived Milford Haven to be broken up.

War Losses

TEMPEST (1942); THORN (1942); TRAVELLER (1942); TROOPER (1943); TURBULENT (1943).

HMS Thrasher (October 1945)

Submarines

"T" CLASS — THIRD GROUP

Ship	Launch Date	Builder
TABARD	21 Nov. 1945	Scotts, Greenock
TACITURN	7 June 1944	Vickers Armstrong, Barrow
TACTICIAN	29 July 1942	Vickers Armstrong, Barrow
TALENT (i)	17 July 1943	Vickers Armstrong, Barrow
TALENT (iii)	13 Feb. 1945	Vickers Armstrong, Barrow
TALLY-HO	23 Dec. 1942	Vickers Armstrong, Barrow
TANTALUS	24 Feb. 1943	Vickers Armstrong, Barrow
TANTIVY	6 April 1943	Vickers Armstrong, Barrow
TAPIR	21 Aug. 1944	Vickers Armstrong, Barrow
TARN	29 Nov. 1944	Vickers Armstrong, Barrow
TASMAN	13 Feb. 1945	Vickers Armstrong, Barrow
TAURUS	27 June 1942	Vickers Armstrong, Barrow
TELEMACHUS	19 June 1943	Vickers Armstrong, Barrow
TEMPLAR	26 Oct. 1942	Vickers Armstrong, Barrow
TEREDO	27 April 1945	Vickers Armstrong, Barrow
THERMOPYLAE	27 June 1945	H.M. Dockyard, Chatham
THOROUGH	30 Oct. 1943	Vickers Armstrong, Barrow
THULE	22 Oct. 1942	H.M. Dockyard, Devonport
TIPTOE	25 Feb. 1944	Vickers Armstrong, Barrow
TIRELESS	19 March 1943	H.M. Dockyard, Portsmouth
TOKEN	19 March 1943	H.M. Dockyard, Portsmouth
TOTEM	28 Sept. 1943	H.M. Dockyard, Devonport
TRADEWIND	11 Dec. 1942	H.M. Dockyard, Chatham
TRENCHANT	24 March 1943	H.M. Dockyard, Chatham
TRESPASSER	29 May 1942	Vickers Armstrong, Barrow
TRUCULENT	12 Sept. 1942	Vickers Armstrong, Barrow
TRUMP	25 March 1944	Vickers Armstrong, Barrow
TRUNCHEON	22 Feb. 1944	H.M. Dockyard, Devonport
TUDOR	23 Sept. 1942	H.M. Dockyard, Devonport
TURPIN	5 Aug. 1944	H.M. Dockyard, Portsmouth

Submarines

"T" CLASS — THIRD GROUP

Displacement (**tons**) 1,090 (surfaced); 1,571 (submerged)
Length 273 ft. 6 ins. **Beam** 26 ft. 6 ins. **Draught** 12 ft. *****Speed**
(**knots**) 15¼ (surfaced); 8¾ (submerged) **Armament** one 4″
gun, one 20 mm A.A., three .303″ **Torpedo Tubes** eleven 21″
(eight forward, two amidships, one aft) seventeen torpedoes
Complement 61.
* *Increases of speed were achieved by those 'T' Class fully
converted. Only marginal improvement in streamlined boats.*

Note:-
The displacement and length was increased in the reconstructed
vessels.
The 4″ gun and five external tubes were removed during reconstruction.

War Losses

P311 (Ex-P91, ex-TUTANKHAMEN) 1943, TERRAPIN (construc-
tive loss) 1945.

Cancelled Orders

THEBAN; TALENT (ii); THREAT; and four un-named boats.
THOR — launched from Portsmouth Dockyard 18 April 1944, but
sold incomplete to E. Rees, Llanelly, in June 1947.
TIARA — launched from Portsmouth Dockyard 18 April 1944, but
sold incomplete to Dover Industries in June, 1947.

Notes

TABARD
14 March 1974 — Towed from Portsmouth, arriving at
Newport to be broken up by J. Cashmore.

TACITURN
8 Aug. 1971 — Sold to T.W. Ward Ltd. and arrived Briton
Ferry to be broken up.

Submarines

Notes

TACTICIAN

6 Dec. 1963   —   Sold to J. Cashmore and arrived Newport to be broken up.

TALENT (i)

1944   —   Sold to Royal Netherlands Navy. Re-named "ZWAARDVIS".

11 Dec. 1962   —   De-commissioned.

15 Jan. 1963   —   Withdrawn from service.

July 1963   —   Sold for scrap to Antwerp Shipbreakers.

TALENT (iii)

April 1945   —   Launched at TASMAN. Re-named TALENT.

28 Feb. 1970   —   Sold to West of Scotland Shipbreaking Co. and arrived Troon for breaking up.

HMS Talent (October 1956)

TALLY-HO

8 Feb. 1967 — Sold to T.W. Ward, Ltd. Towed from Portsmouth, and arrived Briton Ferry on the 10th to be broken up.

TANTALUS

Nov. 1950 — Sold to T.W. Ward Ltd. and arrived Milford Haven to be broken up.

TANTIVY

1951 — Sunk as an A/S target in the Cromarty Firth.

Submarines

Notes

TAPIR

1948-53	—	Loaned to Royal Netherlands and re-named "ZEEHOND".
16 July 1953	—	Returned to Royal Navy.
Feb. 1966	—	Sold to Shipbreaking Industries and arrived Faslane to be broken up.

TARN

1945	—	Sold to Royal Netherlands Navy and re-named "TIJGERHAAI".

TASMAN

April 1945	—	Renamed "TALENT" — see TALENT (iii)

TAURUS

1948	—	Loaned to Royal Netherlands Navy, and re-named "DOLFIJN".
8 Dec. 1953	—	Returned to Royal Navy.
April 1960	—	Sold to Clayton & Davie Ltd. and arrived Dunston-on-Tyne to be broken up.

TELEMACHUS

9 Dec. 1959	—	Arrived Gosport, after 10 years duty with the 4th Submarine Squadron at Sydney, Australia. After a period in the hands of the Naval Construction Research Establishment at Rosyth, for trials, she was sold to Shipbreaking Industries.
Aug. 1961	—	Arrived Charlestown, Fife, to be broken up.

TEMPLAR

1954	—	Sunk in Loch Striven, Scotland, as a target.
4 Dec. 1958	—	Salvaged.
17 July 1959	—	Arrived Troon to be broken up.

Submarines

Notes

TEREDO
5 June 1965   —   Sold T.W. Ward Ltd. and arrived Briton Ferry for breaking up.

THERMOPYLAE
Sept. 1970   —   Sold to West of Scotland Shipbreaking Co., Troon. (See additional notes).

THOROUGH
29 June 1961   —   Sold to Clayton and Davie Ltd. and arrived Dunston-on-Tyne to be broken up.

THULE
14 Sept. 1962   —   Sold to T.W. Ward Ltd. and arrived Inverkeithing to be broken up.

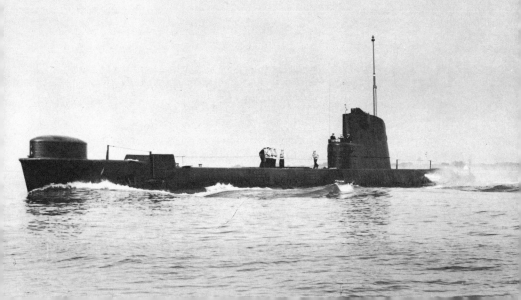

HMS Tiptoe (July 1968)

Submarines

TIPTOE
29 Aug. 1969 —   Paid off at Portsmouth.
1972 —   Sold to Portsmouth Shipbreakers.

TIRELESS
Nov. 1948 —   Sold to J. Cashmore, and arrived Newport to be broken up.

TOKEN
1970 —   Sold to Portsmouth Shipbreakers.

TOTEM
16 June 1965 —   Berthed at Gosport for the last time under the white ensign, prior to transfer to Israel.
Sept. 1967 —   Modernisation in Portsmouth Dockyard was completed.
10 Nov. 1967 —   Commissioned into Israeli Navy, and renamed "DAKAR".
26 Jan. 1968 —   Was lost in Eastern Mediterranean, on passage to Haifa. (See additional notes)

TRADEWIND
14 Dec. 1955 —   Sold to Shipbreaking Industries; arrived Charlestown, Fife to be broken up.

TRENCHANT
23 July 1963 —   Sold to Metal Industries. Arrived Faslane to be broken up.

TRESPASSER
26 Sept. 1961 —   Sold to J.J. King and arrived Gateshead to be broken up.

HMS Totem (May 1953)

TRUCULENT

12 Jan. 1950   —   Sunk in collision with 'DVINA' off the Nore.

14 March 1950   —   Salvaged.

8 May 1950   —   Sold to T.W. Ward for breaking up. (See additional notes).

TRUMP

Aug. 1971   —   Sold to J. Cashmore and arrived Newport to be broken up.

TRUNCHEON

9 Jan. 1968   —   Was handed over to Israeli Navy at Gosport to replace the "DAKAR" (Ex-TOTEM) which had been lost at sea. Was re-named "DOLPHIN".

31 Jan. 1968   —   Arrived in Israel.

Submarines

TUDOR
1 July 1963   —   Sold to Metal Industries.
27 July 1963   —   Arrived at Faslane to be broken up.

TURPIN
1965   —   Transferred to the Israeli Navy, re-named "LEVIATHAN".

Additional Notes

TABARD

Underwent 15 month refit at Cockatoo Dockyard, Sydney, Australia — the first of 3 submarines to do so. Recommissioned there on 27 March 1962.

After 8 years' service with the Royal Australian Navy she left Sydney on 22 March 1968. Arrived Gosport, via Pacific Ocean and Panama Canal, on 11 June.

She spent the next 5 years as a static display ship at H.M.S. Dolphin, having up to 10,000 visitors a year. She was replaced by "ALLIANCE".

TALENT (Ex-Tasman)

Was swept out of dry dock in Chatham Dockyard on 15 December 1954 when the caisson collapsed. She was subsequently reconstructed and "streamlined" with a fin which was damaged in collision with an unknown merchant ship when TALENT was submerged off the Isle of Wight on 8 May 1956.

She made her last dive in the North Sea after a 6 day visit to Sunderland. Paid off in December 1966.

THERMOPYLAE

Was scuttled in Loch Striven, Scotland, and raised as a training exercise for salvage craft. Afterwards beached in Kames Bay.

Arrived at Troon, under tow, on 3 July 1970.

THULE

On 18 November 1960 she was damaged around her fore end when, during exercises in the channel, she surfaced under the R.F.A. Black Ranger — reportedly signalling to the tanker when

HMS Tabard (September 1946)

safely on the surface "Thules rush in where Rangers fear to tread!"

TIPTOE

In September-October 1962 she was engaged in a series of trials off Malta into possibilities of escape from a submarine at extreme depths. One officer and six men ascended from TIPTOE when she was 260 feet down.

At 0900 on 13 July 1965 when 10 miles S.E. of Portland Bill, at periscope depth, she collided with the frigate YARMOUTH. She returned to Gosport under her own power. Repaired by Cammell Laird, Birkenhead.

In February 1969 made a 25th Anniversary visit to her birthplace at Barrow.

She featured in the film "We Dive at Dawn," starring John Mills.

Her anchor, mounted on stone, was erected at Blyth in 1979 commemorating Blyth's links with the Silent Service.

Submarines

Additional Notes

TOKEN

In 1967 she towed the Danish merchant ship "UPNOR" clear of Dubh Artack reef off the west coast of Scotland. After 12 hours the "TOKEN" handed over to the tug "LABRADOR" and "UPNOR" was taken to Belfast for repairs.

"TOKEN" carried out her last dive, off Portland, on 8 September, 1967.

TOTEM

On 26 January, 1968 whilst on passage from the U.K. to Haifa she was lost in the Eastern Mediterranean. A full-scale "Subsmash" routine was carried out but no trace of the Dakar and her crew of 69 was found.

In February, 1969, the Israeli Navy announced that it had recovered a distress buoy from the lost submarine. The buoy was found by an Arab on the beach about four miles north of Khan Yunis in the Gaza Strip, on the Mediterranean Eastern Seaboard. The stern marker buoy carried the words in English 'Dakar' — S.O.S. — finder inform Coast Guard or Police." Her loss remains a mystery.

A Totem Pole was presented to HMS Totem by an Indian tribe in Canada. It was said that if ever the Submarine sailed without its totem it would never return,

The totem was left behind when DAKAR (ex Totem) sailed and is now displayed at the Submarine Museum at HMS Dolphin.

TRUCULENT

Sank after a collision in the Thames Estuary on 12 January 1950. "TRUCULENT" had been carrying out trials after a refit at Chatham Dockyard and was returning to Sheerness. Besides her normal complement of 60 she had a Dockyard party of 18. The "DVINA" was coming down the Thames bound for Ipswich with a cargo of Paraffin. There was some confusion over navigation lights and when the mistake was realised, it was too late to avoid a collision. The few men on the bridge of the submarine were swept into the river leaving about 70 still in her. Those who escaped did so before any rescue boat was in the vicinity. 57 were swept away to drown or die of exposure. Only 15 survivors were picked up — 10 by a boat from the "DVINA" and 5 by the Dutch ship "ALMDIJK".

HMS Truculent (July 1946)

The subsequent Court of Inquiry attributed 75% of the blame to the ''TRUCULENT'' and 25% to the ''DVINA''.

The ''TRUCULENT'' was salvaged on the 14 March — using two ex-German lifting vessels ''ENERGIE'' and ''AUSDAUER''. She was beached at Cheney Spit. On the 16th, the wreck was moved 1,000 yards inshore, half a mile from the coast of Sheppey. There, 10 bodies were recovered. On the 23rd, she was re-floated and towed in to Sheerness Dockyard.

TURPIN

For the second time in 7 years Lady Tovey, wife of Admiral of the Fleet Lord Tovey, named the TURPIN. She did it at her launch and again on 17 September 1951 at Chatham after ''TURPIN's'' reconstruction.

In 1958 having developed engine trouble, she was towed home from Kingston, Jamaica, by the tug ''SAMSONIA'' — 5,200 miles in 29½ days, the longest tow in submarine history. Arrived Devonport on 9 April 1948 and proceeded next day to Portsmouth for repairs.

''TURPIN'' was the last submarine based in Malta-leaving for the U.K. on 9 November 1964. She arrived Portsmouth on the 20th to pay off.

Submarines

'A' CLASS

The 'A' Class although basically an improved "T" Class, was designed to incorporate the many modifications and additions deemed necessary after the war service of other submarines. They were intended for service in the Pacific War, where the greater distances involved required a submarine with a higher surface speed and greater endurance. Special attention to habitability was also made by introducing an air conditioning compartment, into which air was drawn from the whole hull to be treated and then re-circulated.

The development of this new design, in association with the use of welding, enabled construction of hulls, of increased strength, to be speeded up. Preparations were made to go into mass production, but the end of the war in the Pacific curtailed this project. Not one "A" boat was completed in time to carry out a war patrol. "AMPHION", the first of class completed, was running "first of class" trials in Scottish waters on VE-Day.

Of the 46 submarines projected only 16 were completed. Some cancelled vessels, whose hulls were complete, were used for tests to destruction and expended as targets.

In most of the class, the two forward external torpedo tubes were removed when they were re-constructed. The vessels were "streamlined" with an enclosed fin, 26½ feet high. "ARTFUL" in 1955 was the first so fitted, and "AUROCHS" was the only one of the class not converted.

Ship	Launch Date	Builder
ACHERON	25 March 1947	H.M. Dockyard, Chatham
AENEAS	25 Oct. 1945	Cammell Laird, Birkenhead
AFFRAY	12 April 1945	Cammell Laird, Birkenhead
ALARIC	18 Feb. 1946	Cammell Laird, Birkenhead
ALCIDE	12 April 1945	Vickers Armstrong, Barrow
ALDERNEY	25 June 1945	Vickers Armstrong, Barrow
ALLIANCE	28 July 1945	Vickers Armstrong, Barrow
AMBUSH	24 Sept. 1945	Vickers Armstrong, Barrow
AMPION	31 Aug. 1944	Vickers Armstrong, Barrow

Submarines

Ship	Launch Date	Builder
ANCHORITE	22 Jan. 1946	Vickers Armstrong, Barrow
ANDREW	6 April 1946	Vickers Armstrong, Barrow
ARTEMIS	26 Aug. 1946	Scotts — Greenock
ARTFUL	22 May 1947	Scotts — Greenock
ASTUTE	30 Jan. 1945	Vickers Armstrong, Barrow
AURIGA	29 March 1945	Vickers Armstrong, Barrow
AUROCHS	28 July 1945	Vickers Armstrong, Barrow

Displacement (**tons**) 1,120 (surfaced), 1,620 (submerged) **Length** 281 ft. 9 ins. **Beam** 22 ft. 3 ins. **Draught** 17 ft. **Speed** (**knots**) 18½ (surfaced), 8 (submerged) **Armament** one 4″ gun, one 20 mm A.A., three .303″ **Torpedo Tubes** ten 21″ (six forward and four aft), (four of them external), twenty torpedoes, (or 26 mines) **Complement** 61.

HMS Aeneas (April 1954)

Submarines

Notes

ACHERON
Aug. 1972 — Broken up at Newport by J. Cashmore Ltd.

AENEAS
13 Dec. 1974 — Arrived in the Tyne to be broken up by Clayton & Davie Ltd. of Dunston.
(See additional notes)

AFFRAY
16 April 1951 — Founded, in the Hurd Deep in the English Channel. (See additional notes).

ALARIC
5 July 1971 — Sold to T.W. Ward Ltd, and arrived Inverkeithing to be broken up.

ALCIDE
1974 — Sold to A. Draper and Sons Ltd. of Hull, for breaking up.

ALDERNEY
Aug. 1972 — Arrived Cairn Ryan, Scotland, to be broken up by Shipbreaking (Queenborough) Ltd.

ALLIANCE
1981 — Preserved as Submarine Museum Ship at Gosport. (See additional notes).

AMBUSH
5 July 1971 — Sold to T.W. Ward Ltd, and arrived Inverkeithing to be broken up. (See additional notes)

AMPHION
6 July 1971 — Sold to T.W. Ward Ltd., and arrived Inverkeithing to be broken up.

Submarines

ANCHORITE

24 Aug. 1970 — Sold to West of Scotland Shipbreaking Co. Arrived Troon to be broken up. (See additional notes).

ANDREW

31 Dec. 1974 — Paid off to Disposal list.

4 May 1977 — Towed to the Yard at Laira, Plymouth, of Davies & Cann Ltd., to be broken up. (See additional notes).

ARTEMIS

1 July 1971 — Foundered whilst alongside at Gosport.

6 July 1971 — Was raised by salvage vessels "GOLDEN EYE" and "KINLOSS".

1972 — Sold to H.G. Pounds of Portsmouth, for breaking up.

ARTFUL

23 June 1972 — Sold to Shipbreaking (Queenborough) Ltd. to be broken up at Cairnryan.

ASTUTE

1 Oct. 1970 — Sold to Clayton and Davie, Ltd. & arrived Dunston-on-Tyne, to be broken up.

AURIGA

14 Nov. 1974 — Sold to J. Cashmore Ltd. (Newport).

11 Feb. 1975 — Towed from Rosyth for breaking up.

AUROCHS

7 Feb. 1967 — Sold to West of Scotland Shipbreaking Co. & arrived Troon to be broken up.

Submarines

Additional Notes

AENEAS

Was loaned to the Vickers Shipbuilding Group from July to November, 1972. Arrived at their yard at Barrow on 26 July, 1972, to be fitted with SLAM (Submarine Launched Air Missile). She was used to carry out tests of this anti-aircraft missile system. The submarine successfully fired missiles on trials and gave three demonstrations, watched by Royal and Overseas Naval Representatives. "AENEAS" returned to Devonport on 15 November, 1972. The trials were not pursued as the missile had too short a range.

AFFRAY

On 16 April, 1951, she sailed from Portsmouth on a training exercise with 75 men on board. At 2115 she reported that she was diving about 30 miles south of the Isle of Wight. She failed to surface the next morning, as expected about 20 miles south east of Start Point. The "Subsmash" procedure was instigated. 26 ships of four nations joined in the search. Early in the morning of the 18 April it was reported that contact had been made, but, on investigation, was discounted.

On 21 April, the Admiralty announced that all 'A' Class submarines were not to proceed to sea pending investigation into the loss of the "AFFRAY".

A new search began to try and find the "AFFRAY" using underwater camera equipment in H.M.S. RECLAIM. On 14 June, "AFFRAY" was found 67 miles, 228° from St. Catherine's Lighthouse, 37 miles south west of her last reported diving position, in 43 fathoms of water.

Examination after salvage, revealed that her snort tube had fractured, leaving a 10″ hole through the pressure hull. But the actual cause of the tragedy has never been established with any certainty.

ALLIANCE

On 1 October, 1947, she left Portsmouth, with 7 officers and 65 ratings, bound for a record-breaking cruise. Calling at Gibraltar for fuel and water, she sailed into the Atlantic, where on 9 October 1947 she dived to carry out a tropical snort cruise, which was to last until 8 November, 1947. The submarine covered 3,193 miles — sailing S.E. from the Canary Islands to Cape Verde; then

Submarines

Additional Notes

due south; due east along the Equator; N.E. to Cape Palmas; and northwards up the African coast to Freetown. It was done entirely with the use of Snort, with the exception of 3 nights when "ALLIANCE" went deep to take bathythermograph records and to work the batteries.

At 0900 on 8 November, 1947, she surfaced and both conning tower hatches were opened together for the first time in 30 days.

In 1965 she was used to test a new camouflage paint scheme, when in the Far East.

29 July, 1971, was damaged by a battery explosion whilst alongside at Portland.

15 August, 1979 towed from the Gosport submarine base to Southampton where Vosper Ship Repairers Ltd. prepared her for return to Haslar where she was lifted out of the water, and placed on permanent display.

HMS Affray (October 1946)

Submarines

Additional Notes

AMBUSH

On 12 February, 1948, she left the Clyde to carry out a prolonged 'Snort' cruise between Jan Mayen and Bear Islands, returning to the Forth on 18 March, 1948.

This was the third in the series of long snort patrols, first carried out by TACITURN in temperate waters and secondly by ALLIANCE under tropical conditions. Objects were to gain information on physiological problems associated with prolonged snorting; and to deduce suitable economical speeds/fuel consumption, etc., when snorting.

ANCHORITE

Sustained damage forward, on 3 October, 1960, when she struck an uncharted rock at 110 feet in the Hauraki Gulf, off North Island, New Zealand. 'ANCHORITE' was able to surface and reach harbour safely under her own power.

ANDREW

She was the last submarine in the R.N. to carry a deck gun, and was the last submarine, designed during World War 2, to be at sea. Her 26 years of operations included the first ever submerged crossing of the Atlantic, in May 1953, 'Snorting' for 2,500 miles from Bermuda to the English Channel.

Was a 'film star' as U.S.S. SWORDFISH in "On the Beach" with Gregory Peck and Ava Gardner. Also appeared as a German submarine in the B.B.C.T/V series "Warship".

On 18 December, 1968, she arrived at Portsmouth after 10 years in the Far East.

In 1973, she was 'caught' by the Teignmouth trawler "EMMA WILL", in her nets. The trawler was towed stern first and called for help before "ANDREW" broke out of the nets.

The final months of her service were spent as a 'target' to train anti-submarine ships and aircraft.

In December, 1974, she made a farewell visit to London, before returning to Devonport on the 18th to pay off.

Attempts to preserve her failed and she was finally scrapped by Davis and Cann Ltd., at Plymouth in 1977.

ARTEMIS

In 1954 the Admiralty Security Police investigated a suspected

HMS Andrew (April 1969)

Submarines

case of sabotage on board "ARTEMIS". A stoker mechanic from the Submarine School was sentenced to 1 year's detention on 2 charges of placing signal grenades in the engine.

"ARTEMIS" was the cause of a "Subsmash" alarm in 1963 when late surfacing in the Atlantic in response to signals. Canadian planes and ships started a big rescue operation, 700 miles east of New York, but "ARTEMIS" surfaced safely 1½ hours later. She was then on loan to the Canadian Government, but operating with a mainly British crew.

On 1 July 1971, "ARTEMIS" sank alongside the jetty at Fort Blockhouse Gosport having been moved there by tug from dry dock. The accident happened whilst "First Filling" her fuel tanks with salt water, prior to fuelling the ship. Water poured into the vessel through an open hatch. Attempts to halt the flooding failed because a shore power cable rigged through the hatchway prevented it being closed. Twelve men managed to scramble to safety but three were trapped in a forward compartment underwater for several hours.

The cause of the accident was deemed to have been "because too many people had forgotten basic principles of submarine safety — ship stability!"

AURIGA

During night exercises off Gibraltar on 11/12 February, 1970, a battery explosion occurred in the fore end beneath the ratings' accommodation. The explosion injured 10 ratings, but none seriously. The "AURIGA" managed to 'limp' back to Gibraltar.

AUROCHS

Returned to Gosport on 3 December, 1958, after 12,000 mile voyage from Australia via the Pacific. She had left U.K. in January, 1956, and sailed, via the Mediterranean, to join the 4th Submarine Squadron at Sydney. She thus became the second British submarine to circumnavigate the world.

"AUROCHS" was surveyed in September, 1964, and found to be in such poor condition that it was considered not worth refitting her. She lay at Gosport, apparently in Reserve, although officially in commission, until 9 May, 1966 when she was towed to Devonport for de-storing. Left Plymouth on 4 February 1967, for Troon.

HMS Artemis (March 1960)

Submarines

HMS/M METEORITE

After the surrender of Germany in 1945, seventeen of her submarines were allocated to the Royal Navy.

Eight of them U249, U776, U1023, U1105, U1171, U1407, U3017 and U2326 were temporarily commissioned into the Royal Navy for experimental purposes; and one, U190, to the Royal Canadian Navy.

Two were trasnferred to the French Navy, and four to the Royal Norwegian Navy.

The remaining vessels were scuttled or scrapped.

U-1407 was a Walter-type submarine built in 1944 by Blohm and Voss.

Displacement (tons) 312 (surfaced); 357 (submerged) **Length overall** 136 ft. 3 ins. **Beam** 11 ft. 3 ins. **Draught** 14 ft. **Speed (knots)** 8½ (surfaced); 5 (submerged); 25 (designed) **Armament** two 21″ torpedo tubes, forward.
Complement 19.

A German tug, bound for London as part of the war reparations, towed U-1407 to Sheerness, where a British ocean-going tug completed the tow to the yard of Vickers Armstrong Ltd at Barrow-in-Furness.

There she was rebuilt and commissioned as HMS METEORITE. To supervise the reconstruction, Professor Walter and his staff came from Germany to Barrow to advise during the rebuilding.

During further modifications carried out at Barrow in October, 1948, "METEORITE" was fitted with a modified conning tower.

"METEORITE" was broken up in September 1949 by T.W. Ward Ltd, at Barrow.

Photo: By permission RN
Submarine Museum.

HMS Meteorite

Submarines

EXPERIMENTAL TYPE

Ship	Launch Date	Builder
EXCALIBUR	25 Feb. 1955	Vickers Armstrong, Barrow
EXPLORER	5 March 1954	Vickers Armstrong, Barrow

Displacement (tons) 780 (surfaced); c. 1,000 (submerged) **Length** 225 ft. 6 ins. **Beam** 15 ft. 8 ins. **Draught** 11 ft. **Speed** more than 25 submerged **Complement** 41 (EXCALIBUR); 49 (EXPLORER).

Notes

EXCALIBUR
Jan. 1965   —   Disposal List (Scrap).
5 Feb. 1970   —   Sold to T.W. Ward Ltd & towed from Barrow to be broken up.

EXPLORER
1963   —   Was found not to be worth refitting & sold to T.W. Ward Ltd.
8 Feb. 1965   —   Handed over at Barrow for breaking up.

Additional Notes

These entirely experimental submarines were evolved from U-1407 (H.M.S. METEORITE), and were built to assess the practical problems in running hydrogen-peroxide submarines.

They were a new streamlined type, designed for high underwater speed. They had a modern version of battery and main motors for underwater propulsion, but additional to diesel electric machinery, were fitted with turbine machinery for which energy was supplied by burning diesel fuel in decomposed hydrogen peroxide. They were amongst the fastest submarines in the world.

"EXPLORER" was the first submarine to be launched for the Royal Navy since the completion of the 'A' Class in 1948.

Both boats provided valuable training experience for airborne and surface anti-submarine forces but the advent of the nuclear submarine soon rendered them obsolete.

HMS Explorer (March 1957)

Submarines

MIDGET SUBMARINES

This class of vessel was built, during World War 2, for attacking enemy warships moored in protected anchorages. (Specifically TIRPITZ). They were towed to the vicinity of the target, often by a conventional submarine, and then released.

Early boats were built for trials and training purposes before the X series were built for operations. All these were lost or scrapped by 1945, except for X24 which was preserved on blocks at the Submarine Base, HMS Dolphin, at Gosport.

A further 6 training vessels, XT series, were built by Vickers Armstrong, Barrow, but were scrapped soon after the end of the war.

The following XE boats continued in service for a few post-war years.

XE CLASS

Ship	Launch Date	Builder
XE 1 to XE 6	See below	Vickers Armstrong, Barrow
XE 7	" "	Broadbent, Huddersfield
XE 8	" "	Broadbent, Huddersfield
XE 9	" "	Marshall, Gainsborough
XE 10	" "	Marshall Gainsborough
XE 11	" "	Markham, Chesterfield
XE 12	" "	Markham, Chesterfield

Note: All built between December 1943 and April 1945.

Displacement (**tons**) 30¼ (surfaced); 33½ (submerged) **Length** 53 ft. 3 ins. **Beam** 5 ft. 9 ins. **Draught** 5 ft. 9 ins. **Speed** (**knots**) 6½ (surfaced); 5½ (submerged) **Armament** 2 × 2 ton ''side-cargoes'' (delayed action bottom mines and/or limpet mines) **Complement** 4 (3 in separate passage crew).

Notes

XE 1 to XE 6

Ordered from V.A. Barrow, but cancelled.

Submarines

Notes

XE 7	Discarded in 1953.

XE 8	1945 —	Sank in tow off Portland.
	May 1973 —	Was salvaged. It was intended she be put on display in London, but in 1981 she still lay derelict at the Imperial War Museum, Duxford, near Cambridge.

XE 9	1955 —	Discarded and allocated to H.M.S. VERNON for bottom trials.

XE 10	Ordered from Marshall's, but cancelled.

XE 11		
6 March, 1945	—	Lost in collision with boom defence vessel at Loch Striven. Was salvaged and broken up.

XE 12	1952 —	Scrapped, after being cannabalised for spares.

HMS XE7 (September 1946)

Submarines

MIDGET SUBMARINES—"IMPROVED TYPES"

After the great success of the earlier types, four "improved" boats were built in 1954-55.

They basically comprised four compartments — a battery room; a "wet and dry" compartment (Lock) from which the diver left to cut nets or attach limpet mines; a control room; and an engine room.

Ship	Launch Date	Builder
STICKLEBACK X 51	1 Oct. 1954	Vickers Armstrong, Barrow
SHRIMP X 52	30 Dec. 1954	Vickers Armstrong, Barrow
SPRAT X 53	1 March 1954	Vickers Armstrong, Barrow
MINNOW X 54	5 May 1955	Vickers Armstrong, Barrow

Displacement (tons) 35 **Length overall** 53 ft 10½ ins. **Beam** 6 ft. 3½ ins. **Armament** 2 explosive charges **Complement** 5 (3 in passage crew).

HMS Stickleback (May 1955)

HMS Shrimp (October 1956)

Notes

STICKLEBACK

15 July 1958   —   Handed over to Royal Swedish Navy at Portland. Re-named "SPIGGEN", (Swedish equivalent of STICKLEBACK). Used as target during A/S exercises and to train harbour defences against attack by enemy midget submarines. Transported from Sweden back to Devonport in R.F.A. RESURGENT. Now at Imperial War Museum, at Duxford near Cambridge.

SHRIMP & MINNOW

1961   —   Disposal List.

1965   —   Broken up in Rosyth Dockyard.

SPRAT

       Loaned to U.S. Navy to take part in trials in testing harbour defences.

20 June 1958   —   Loaded aboard U.S. transport ALCOR at Portsmouth, for Norfolk, VA. During tests was manned by R.N.

13 Sept. 1958   —   Returned to Portsmouth, aboard U.S.S. ANTARES.

1961   —   Disposal List   —

1965   —   Broken up in Rosyth Dockyard.

Submarines

"PORPOISE CLASS"

These were the first operational submarines, designed since World War 2, to be accepted into service. There were to have been more boats in the class, but the project was dropped when the decision was taken to develop nuclear powered submarines.

They were propelled by diesel electric drive from Admiralty Standard Range Diesels and from large batteries driving motors when the boats were submerged. Increased battery power gave them higher underwater speed and improved diving depths were achieved by virtue of greater hull strength.

Although limited in their submerged speed and endurance compared with nuclear submarines, conventional (or patrol) classes still have an important role to play.

Ship	Launch Date	Builder
CACHALOT	11 Dec. 1957	Scotts — Greenock
FINWHALE	21 July 1959	Cammell Laird, Birkenhead
GRAMPUS	30 May 1957	Cammell Laird, Birkenhead
NARWHAL	25 Oct. 1957	Vickers Armstrong, Barrow
PORPOISE	25 April 1956	Vickers Armstrong, Barrow
RORQUAL	5 Dec. 1956	Vickers Armstrong, Barrow
SEALION	31 Dec. 1959	Cammell Laird, Birkenhead
WALRUS	22 Sept. 1959	Scotts — Greenock

Displacement (**tons**) 1,605 (surfaced); 2,405 (submerged) **Length** 295 ft. 3 ins. **Beam** 26 ft. 6 ins. **Draught** 18 ft. **Speed** (**knots**) 12 (surfaced); 17 (submerged) **Armament** conventional and homing torpedoes **Torpedo Tubes** eight 21", internal (6 bow and 2 stern) **Complement** 71.

Submarines

Notes

CACHALOT
2 Sept. 1977	—	Paid off for disposal, at Devonport. Sale to Egypt was cancelled.
14 Feb. 1980	—	Arrived at Blyth, to be broken up by Blyth Shipbreakers & Repairers Ltd.

FINWHALE
6 Nov. 1978	—	Paid off for Disposal but retained for harbour training at Gosport.

GRAMPUS
4 Dec. 1978	—	Placed on Disposal List (Scrap).
29 Feb. 1980	—	Removed from Disposal List — being converted by Portsmouth Dockyard into a static ASW target.

HMS Porpoise (April 1971)

Submarines

Notes

NARWHAL
2 June 1980   —   Sunk off Portland.
26 June 1980   —   Raised again as a salvage exercise by Swedish heavy lift ship "HEBE III" and two RMAS vessels.

PORPOISE
1981   —   Still in commission.

RORQUAL
5 May 1977   —   Towed to Plymouth yard of Davies and Cann Ltd., for breaking up.

SEALION
1981   —   Still in commission.

WALRUS
1981   —   Still in commission.

Additional Notes

PORPOISE
In 1979 assumed the role of target for the Admiralty's new underwater weapons. She was modified to strengthen her ballast tanks, shafts and main vents, because some of the weapons fired at her were meant to hit — without, of course, the explosive charge.

RORQUAL
When off Mozambique in 1966, two members of the crew lost their lives in an engine room explosion. "RORQUAL" reached Durban on 2 September.

OBERON CLASS. All completed in 1959/64 & remain in service. For details of these and the modern nuclear submarines in service in the R.N. see "British Warships & Auxiliaries".

HMS Finwhale (September 1964)

Submarine Depot Ships

Ship	Launch Date	Builder
MONTCLARE	18 Dec. 1921	John Brown & Co. Ltd. Clydebank
WOLFE (Ex-Montcalm)	3 July 1920	John Brown & Co. Ltd. Clydebank

Displacement 19,600 tons **Length** 575 ft. **Beam** 70 ft. **Draught** 28ft. **Speed** 17 knots **Armament** four 4″, nineteen 20mm **Complement** 480 (including repair staff).

Notes

MONTCLARE

Former Canadian Pacific Liner, converted into a Destroyer Depot Ship in 1944, but again converted into a Submarine Depot Ship after the war.

1948	—	Captain (Submarines), 3rd Submarine Flotilla.
Feb 1955	—	Laid up at Portsmouth.
28 Jan. 1958	—	Left Portsmouth in tow for Inverkeithing to be broken up.

WOLFE

1946-47	—	Captain (Submarines) 1st Submarine Flotilla.
1949	—	Paid Off.
8 Nov. 1952	—	Arrived Faslane for breaking up.

HMS Montclare (March 1946)

Submarine Depot Ships

Ship	Launch Date	Builder
MAIDSTONE	21 Oct. 1937	John Brown & Co. Ltd. Clydebank.

Displacement 8,900 tons **Length** 574 ft. **Beam** 73 ft. **Draught** 20 ft. **Speed** 17 knots **Armament** eight 4.5″, eight 2 PDR. pompoms, five 40mm AA, eight 20mm AA, two 2 PDR. **Complement** 502.

Notes

MAIDSTONE

1956-58	—	Flagship of Commander-in-Chief, Home Fleet.
April 1958	—	Paid off after being in continuous service for 20 years.
1958-62	—	Extensively reconstructed at Portsmouth to enable her to support nuclear powered submarines — 4.5″ guns removed.
1962	—	Sailed for the Clyde to support 3rd Submarine Squadron. Depot Ship for submarines at Faslane.
23 Jan. 1968	—	Sailed to join the Reserve Fleet at Rosyth.
Oct. 1969	—	Recommissioned as Accommodation ship for troops sent to Belfast. Later used as a floating prison.
1977	—	Towed to Rosyth on being given up by the Army.
23 May 1978	—	Towed to Inverkeithing to be broken up.

HMS Maidstone (January 1946)

Submarine Depot Ships

Ship	Launch Date	Builder
FORTH	11 Aug. 1938	John Brown & Co. Ltd. Clydebank

Displacement 9,060 tons **Length** 574 ft. **Beam** 73 ft. **Draught** 20 ft. **Speed** 17 knots **Armameant** eight 4.5″, two multiple pom-poms, four 3 PDR **Complement** 502.

Notes

FORTH

1953	—	Provided relief for Greek earthquake victims.
1956	—	Headquarters of Naval Officer-in-Charge, Port Said during the Suez crisis.
Oct. 1960	—	Returned to Devonport after nearly thirteen years in the Mediterranean, where she had been Depot Ship for Submarines and Coastal Minesweepers.
1962-66	—	Extensively reconstructed at Chatham to enable her to support nuclear powered submarines.
7 June 1971	—	Arrived Devonport from Far East after five years based at Singapore with the Seventh Submarine Squadron.
17 Feb. 1972	—	Re-named DEFIANCE. Depot Ship of Devonport Fleet Maintenance Base and Parent Ship of 2nd Submarine Squadron.
May 1978	—	When DEFIANCE personnel moved into offices ashore, FORTH was placed on Disposal List.

HMS Forth (June 1953)

Submarine Depot Ships

Ship	Launch Date	Builder
ADAMANT	30 Nov. 1940	Harland & Wolff Ltd. Belfast.

Displacement 12,500 tons **Length** 658 ft. **Beam** 70 ft. 6 ins. **Draught** 20 ft. **Speed** 17 knots **Armament** eight 4.5″ (later removed), sixteen 2 PDR, four 40mm AA, ten 20mm AA, four 3 PDR. **Complement** 750.

Notes

ADAMANT

1950	—	Paid off.
Oct. 1954	—	Commissioned.
1955-57	—	H.Q. Ship of 3rd Submarine Squadron.
1959-62	—	H.Q. Ship of 3rd Submarine Squadron.
1964-65	—	H.Q. Ship of 2nd Submarine Squadron.
June 1966	—	Placed on Sales List.
Sept. 1970	—	Arrived Inverkeithing for breaking up.

HMS Adamant (June 1953)

Depot Ships

Ship	Launch Date	Builder
WOODBRIDGE HAVEN (Ex-Loch Torridon)	13 Jan. 1945	Swan Hunter & Wigham Richardson, Wallsend

Displacement 1,652 tons **Length** 307 ft. 4 ins. **Beam** 38 ft. 6 ins. **Draught** 12 ft. 9 ins. **Speed** 19.5 knots **Armament** one 4″, six 20mm AA **Complement** 103.

Notes

WOODBRIDGE HAVEN

		Built as a Frigate but converted to a Submarine Depot Ship.
1946-54	—	Used as Submarine Target Ship.
1955	—	Commissioned as Headquarters Ship of 2nd Minesweeping Squadron.
1957	—	Captain Minesweepers, Mediterranean.
1958-60	—	Captain Inshore Flotilla, Mediterranean.
1960-63	—	Captain Inshore Flotilla, Far East.
1963	—	Paid Off.
9 Aug. 1965	—	Left Portsmouth in tow for Blyth to be broken up.

DEPOT AND REPAIR SHIP FOR COASTAL CRAFT

Ship	Launch Date	Builder
DERBY HAVEN (Ex-Loch Assynt)	14 Dec. 1944	Swan Hunter & Wigham Richardson, Wallsend

Displacement 1,652 tons **Length** 307 ft. 4 ins. **Beam** 38ft. 6 ins. **Draught** 12 ft. 9 ins. **Speed** 19.5 knots **Armament** two 4″, six 20mm **Complement** 140.

Notes

DERBY HAVEN

30 July 1949	—	Transferred to the Persian Navy and renamed BABR.
1969	—	Paid off and laid up in the Persian Gulf to await disposal.

REPLENISHMENT SHIP [RN]

Ship	Launch Date	Builder
BULAWAYO (Ex-German Nordmark, ex-Northmark)	5 Oct. 1937	Schichau, Elbing

Displacement 15,000 tons **Length** 584 ft. **Beam** 72 ft. 6 ins. **Draught (maximum)** 30 ft. 3 ins. **Speed** 21 knots **Armament** two 4″ AA, four 40mm AA, two 20mm AA **Complement** 292.

Notes

BULAWAYO

	Allocated to Britain by the Inter-Allied Repatriation Commission.
8 June 1945 —	Arrived Rosyth.
June 1945-Nov. 1945 —	Conversion at Palmer's Yard, Hebburn, but afterwards paid off into Reserve.
Jan. 1946 —	Renamed Northmark, placed in Reserve at Milford Haven.
May 1946 —	In Reserve at Falmouth.
1947 —	Approval for her to serve as H.M. Ship.
July 1947 —	At Portsmouth for refit.
Feb. 1948 —	Used for Oil Freighting to and from Trinidad.
July 1948 —	At Chatham for refit.
Oct. 1948 —	At Portsmouth for refit.
Oct. 1949 —	In the Mediterranean.
Jan. 1950 —	At Chatham for refit.
Feb.-Mar.1950 —	In the Mediterranean.
May 1950 —	In the Gareloch to act as H.Q. ship Reserve Fleet, Clyde.
Oct. 1950 —	In Reserve.
1954 —	Living Ship at Faslane.
1955 —	Reduced to Care & Maintenance.
Sept. 1955 —	For Disposal.
4 Oct. 1955 —	Arrived Dalmuir for breaking up.

Depot Ships

Ship	Launch Date	Builder
AUSONIA	22 March 1921	Armstrong Whitworth & Co. Ltd., Newcastle-on-Tyne
ARTIFEX (Ex-Aurania)	6 Feb. 1924	Swan Hunter Ltd.
ALAUNIA	7 Feb. 1925	John Brown & Co. Ltd., Clydebank.

Displacement 19,000 tons **Length** 538 ft. **Beam** 65 ft. 3 ins. **Draught (maximum)** 32 ft. 4 ins. **Speed** 15 knots **Armament** several 20mm AA **Complement** 592.

Notes

AUSONIA

Former Cunard Transatlantic Liner, which became an Armed Merchant Cruiser, then a Heavy Repair Ship in World War II.

16 Sept. 1958	—	Commissioned At Devonport to relieve HMS Ranpura after 12 months in reserve.
1963	—	Captain Submarines and Minesweepers in the Mediterranean.
1964	—	Captain Submarines, Fifth S/M Division
18 Aug. 1964	—	Returned to Portsmouth from Malta & sold to Spanish Shipbreakers
13 Sept. 1965	—	Left Portsmouth for Castellon.

ARTIFEX

1947-48	—	Training Ship at Rosyth.
1955	—	Paid off into Reserve.
28 Dec. 1960	—	Sold to Italian Shipbreakers.
7 Jan. 1961	—	Left Rosyth for Spezia.

ALAUNIA

1949-57	—	In Service as Static Training Ship for Engine Room Ratings at Devonport.
10 Sept. 1957	—	Arrived Blyth for breaking up.

HMS Ausonia (August 1964)

Destroyer Depot Ships

Ship	Launch Date	Builder
WOOLWICH	20 Sept. 1934	Fairfield Shipbuilding & Eng. Co. Ltd., Govan.

Displacement 8,750 tons **Length** 575 ft. **Beam** 64 ft. **Draught** 14 ft. 8 ins. **Speed** 15 knots **Armament** four 4" AA, ten smaller guns **Complement** 406.

Notes

WOOLWICH

1947	—	Flag Officer, Mediterranean Fleet Destroyers.
1948	—	Maintainance/Accommodation ship Reserve Ships at Harwich.
1952	—	Rosyth refit thence to Gareloch.
1957	—	Rosyth refit thence to Devonport as accommodation ship 1958-1962.
Oct. 1962	—	Sold to Arnott Young to be broken up at Dalmuir.

HMS Woolwich (May 1937)

Destroyer Depot Ships

Ship	Launch Date	Builder
TYNE	28 Feb. 1940	Scotts Shipbuilding & Eng. Co., Greenock

Displacement 11,000 tons **Length** 621 ft. **Beam** 66 ft. **Draught** 20 ft. **Speed** 17 knots **Armament** eight 4.5″, two multiple pom-poms.

Notes

TYNE

1947-48	—	In Reserve. Senior Officer's Ship, Reserve Fleet, Harwich.
1950-52	—	Flag Officer Destroyers, Mediterranean Fleet.
1954	—	Fifth Cruiser Squadron Flagship and Flag Officer Second-in-Command, Far East.
1955-56	—	Flagship of C. in C., Home Fleet.
1956-58	—	Refitted.
1958	—	Flagship of C. in C., Home Fleet.
1959-60	—	Flag Officer Flotillas, Home Fleet.
1961	—	Accommodation Ship for Fleet Maitnenance Unit at Portsmouth.
18 July, 1961	—	Towed to Devonport, where she was placed in Reserve and used as a Living Ship.
1969	—	Headquarters Ship of Fleet Maintenance Unit, Devonport.
1972	—	Replaced by the "Forth" and placed on Disposal List.
1972	—	Broken up at Barrow.

Note:- Sister Ship Hecla was a War Loss, 1942.

HMS Tyne (May 1959)

Escort Maintenance Ships

HEAD CLASS

Ship	Launch Date	Builder
BEACHY HEAD	27 Sept. 1944	Burrard Dry Dock Co. North Vancouver
FLAMBOROUGH HEAD	7 Oct. 1944	Burrard Dry Dock Co. North Vancouver
BERRY HEAD	21 Oct. 1944	North Vancouver, Ship Repairs
DUNCANSBY HEAD	17 Nov. 1944	Burrard Dry Dock Co. North Vancouver
RAME HEAD	22 Nov. 1944	Burrard Dry Dock Co. North Vancouver

Displacement 8,580 tons **Length** 439 ft. **Beam** 62 ft. **Draught** 29 ft. **Speed** 11 knots **Armament** sixteen to thirty-two 20mm AA **Complement** 440.

Notes

BEACHY HEAD

1947	—	Lent to R. Netherlands Navy and re-named VULKAAN.
1950	—	Returned to R.N. and assumed original name.
1952	—	Acquired by R. Canadian Navy.
1953	—	Re-named CAPE SCOTT.
1957	—	In Reserve.
28 Jan. 1959	—	Commissioned at Halifax as Mobile Repair Ship.
1971	—	Paid Off.
1972	—	De-commissioned but remained in alongside service.
1977	—	Sold.

HMS Rame Head (July 1962)

Escort Maintenance Ships

Notes

FLAMBOROUGH HEAD

1951	—	Transferred to Canada.
31 Jan. 1953	—	Re-named CAPE BRETON and commissioned as Training Ship for Artificers until 1958.
1958-59	—	Converted at Esquimault.
16 Nov. 1959	—	Commissioned as Mobile Repair Ship.
10 Feb. 1964	—	Paid off into Reserve.
1972	—	De-commissioned but remained in alongside service.

BERRY HEAD

1947-50	—	Senior Officer's Ship, Reserve Fleet, Sheerness.
1951	—	Paid Off.
1960-63	—	Refitted and modernised.
1968-69	—	Refitted to relieve TRIUMPH in the Far East. Commissioned Jan. 1969.
1970	—	Returned to U.K.
1971	—	Refitted at Devonport.
1972	—	In Reserve at Chatham.
1976	—	Disposal List. But still (1981) in use as Dockyard Accommodation ship at Devonport.

DUNCANSBY HEAD

1957	—	In Reserve.
1 Dec. 1962	—	Became part of HMS COCHRANE as a living ship with GIRDLE NESS (S.O.R.S., Rosyth).
1967-69	—	Harbour Accomodation Ship, Rosyth.
1969	—	Broken up in Spain.

RAME HEAD

1960-63	—	Refitted and modernised.
1963	—	Living ship for Senior Officer Reserve Ships, Portsmouth.

Maintenance Ship

Ship	Launch Date	Builder
PORTLAND BILL	18 May 1945	Burrard Dry Dock Co. Ltd. North Vancouver

Displacement 8,580 tons **Length** 425 ft. **Beam** 57 ft. **Draught** 25 ft. **Speed** 17 knots **Armament** sixteen 20mm AA.

Notes

1947	—	In Reserve Fleet.
Jan. 1951	—	Sold to the Stag Line and re-named ZINNIA.

Depot Ship for Coastal Craft

Ship	Launch Date	Builder
CAPE WRATH	24 Aug. 1945	West Coast Shipbuilding Co. Ltd., Vancouver B.C.

Displacement 8,755 tons **Length** 439 ft. **Beam** 62 ft. **Draught** 29 ft. **Speed** 11 knots.

Notes

1947	—	In Reserve Fleet.
1951	—	Sold to commercial interests and re-named MARINE FORTUNE.

Maintenance Ships

MULL CLASS

Ship	Launch Date	Builder
MULL OF GALLOWAY (Ex-Kinnard Head)	26 Oct. 1944	North Vancouver Ship Repairs Ltd.
MULL OF KINTYRE	5 April 1945	North Vancouver Ship Repairs Ltd.

Displacement 8,500 **Length** 441 ft. 6 ins. **Beam** 57 ft. 6 ins. **Draught** 20 ft. 3 ins. **Speed** 11 knots **Armament** sixteen 20mm

Notes

MULL OF GALLOWAY

1947	—	In Reserve.
1947-49	—	Headquarters ship of Senior Officer, Reserve Fleet, Clyde.
1950	—	Paid Off.
1954	—	Re-commissioned to become Inshore Minesweeping Flotilla Headquarters Ship.
1957	—	In Reserve.
16 Feb. 1965	—	Left Portsmouth in tow bound for Hamburg to be broken up.

MULL OF KINTYRE

1950	—	Paid Off.
1955	—	Brought forward as Armament Maintenance Ship, but later became Repair and Accommodation Ship.
Aug. 1961	—	Completed conversion to Minesweeper Maintenance Ship for service at Singapore.
1962-67	—	Commanding Officer of Reserve Ships, Singapore.
Dec. 1969		Sold to Hong Kong Shipbreakers. She broke away from her tow on 19 Dec. 1969, but was re-covered and towed to Manila

HMS Mull of Kintyre (December 1948)

Maintenance Ships

NESS CLASS

Ship	Launch Date	Builder
BUCHAN NESS	10 Feb. 1945	West Coast Shipbuilding Co. Ltd. Vancouver
GIRDLE NESS	29 March 1945	Burrard Dry Dock Co. Vancouver

Displacement 8,580 tons **Length** 441 ft. **Beam** 57 ft. **Draught** 21 ft. **Speed** 10 knots **Complement** 440.

Notes

BUCHAN NESS

1950	—	Paid off.
25 Sept. 1959	—	Arrived Faslane for breaking up.

GIRDLE NESS

1946	—	Paid Off.
1947-53	—	In Reserve. With DODMAN POINT formed COCHRANE at Rosyth.
Oct. 1953 -July 1956	—	Converted at Devonport Dockyard to a Guided Weapons Trials Ship, mounting a triple launcher for "Seaslug".
1959-61	—	In the Mediterranean.
5 Dec. 1961	—	Paid off as G.W. Trials Ship, at Devonport.
1 Dec. 1962	—	Recommissioned to perform, (with DUNCANSBY HEAD) function of Barracks and Base Supply Depot at Rosyth as H.M.S. COCHRANE.
1963	—	In Reserve.
1967-70	—	Harbour Accomodation Ship at Rosyth, along with DUNCANSBY HEAD.
11 Aug. 1970	—	Arrived Faslane for breaking up.

HMS Girdle Ness (June 1957)

Landing Ship Maintenance Ships

POINT CLASS

Ship	Launch Date	Builder
HARTLAND POINT	4 Nov. 1944	Burrard Dry Dock Co. Ltd. North Vancouver.
DODMAN POINT	14 April 1945	Burrard Dry Dock Co. Ltd. North Vancouver.

Displacement 8,500 tons **Length** 441 ft. **Beam** 57 ft. **Draught** 21 ft. **Speed** 11 knots **Armament** eleven 40mm AA **Complement** 445.

Notes

HARTLAND POINT

1947	—	In Reserve.
1948-51	—	In the Gareloch as the Headquarters Ship of Senior Officer Landing Ships and Craft.
1952	—	Paid Off.
1959-60	—	Extensively refitted as Escort Maintenance Ship.
18 May 1965	—	Returned to Portsmouth from service in Far East.
1972	—	In Reserve. Used as Accommodation Ship in Londonderry.
1974	—	Sold to Marine Oil Industry Repairs Ltd. and converted to an oil rig Repair Ship — but never used as such.
15 Dec. 1978	—	Towed from Mersey to Santander (Spain) for breaking up.

DODMAN POINT

1947	—	With GIRDLE NESS formed COCHRANE at Rosyth.
1948	—	In Reserve.
16 April 1963	—	Arrived Spezia for breaking up.

HMS Hartland Point (May 1960)

Heavy Repair Ships

Ship	Launch Date	Builder
RESOURCE	27 Nov. 1928	Vickers Armstrong, Ltd. Barrow-in-Furness

Displacement 12,300 tons **Length** 500 ft. **Beam** 83 ft. **Draught** (**maximum**) 22 ft. 4 ins. **Speed** 15 knots **Armament** four 4″ AA, four smaller guns **Complement** 450.

Notes

RESOURCE

1946-50	—	Senior Officer's Ship, Reserve Fleet, Portsmouth.
1951	—	Paid Off.
Feb. 1954	—	Sold to T.W. Ward, Inverkeithing for breaking up.

HMS Resource (May 1932)

Heavy Repair Ships

Ship	Launch Date	Builder
RANPURA	13 Sept. 1924	R. & W. Hawthorn Leslie Hebburn-on-Tyne

Displacement 16,120 tons **Length** 570 ft. 3 ins. **Beam** 71 ft. 3 ins. **Draught** 28 ft. 3 ins **Speed** 17 knots **Armament** Twenty 20mm. **Complement** 600.

Notes

RANPURA

Former P. & O. Liner converted in 1945 into a Heavy Repair Ship.

Sister ship of A.M.C. RAWALPINDI, which was sunk by SCHARNHORST in 1939.

1947-48	—	Attached M.T.E., Rosyth.
1953-56	—	Flag Officer Flotillas, Mediterranean.
1956-59	—	Senior Officer Ship's, Reserve Fleet, Malta.
1959	—	In Reserve.
April 1961	—	Sold to Italian interests.
25 May 1961	—	Arrived Spezia for breaking up.

HMS Ranpura (April 1946)

Netlayers

Ship	Launch Date	Builder
GUARDIAN	1 Sept. 1932	Chatham Dockyard
PROTECTOR	20 Aug. 1936	Yarrow & Co. Ltd. Scotstown

Displacement 2,860 tons (Protector was later increased to 3,450 tons) **Length** 338 ft. **Beam** 53 ft. **Draught** 11 ft. 6 ins. **Speed** 20 knots **Armament** two 4″, eight 20mm.

Notes

GUARDIAN

		Designed for Netlaying and Fleet Photography.
1947-61	—	In Reserve.
Dec. 1962	—	Arrived Troon for breaking up.

PROTECTOR

		Designed for Netlaying and Target Towing.
1955	—	Refitted for service in Falkland Islands Dependencies.
1959	—	Reclassified as Ice Patrol Ship. As such made an annual visit to the Antarctic. Her last homecoming was in 1968.
1970	—	Broken up at Inverkeithing.

HMS Protector (October 1955)

Did you see Part One of British Warships since 1945?

Introduced by Admiral Sir Guy Grantham, KCB, CBE, DSO. Part One of this series covers Battleships, Aircraft Carriers, Cruisers & Monitors. Copies are available direct from the publishers — £2.15 (incl. postage).

Next in this series . . .

**BRITISH WARSHIPS
SINCE 1943
PART 3 — DESTROYERS**

Write if you wish to be advised of its publication date.